About the Author

I am a professional French Polisher. I started as an apprentice in London Road, West Thurrock, Essex, when I was sixteen. I worked on board cruise ships in different countries, as well as the Bahamas. Through the Covid-19 pandemic, I found that my work was scarce. While I was not working, I found the time to write this story. I have based Li'l Kev on myself as I love to play casual golf. I was brought up in Aveley, Essex and I now live in Suffolk. I have two children and four granddaughters. I am now looking towards my retirement

To Kirsty, Happy Birthday, from Lee (Kevin Lamb)

23-1-24

Li'l Kev
(Life As a Golf Ball)

Levin Kamb

Li'l Kev
(Life As a Golf Ball)

Olympia Publishers
London

www.olympiapublishers.com
OLYMPIA PAPERBACK EDITION

Copyright © Levin Kamb 2023

The right of Levin Kamb to be identified as author of
this work has been asserted in accordance with sections 77 and 78
of the Copyright, Designs and Patents Act 1988.

All Rights Reserved

No reproduction, copy or transmission of this publication
may be made without written permission.
No paragraph of this publication may be reproduced,
copied or transmitted save with the written permission of the
publisher, or in accordance with the provisions
of the Copyright Act 1956 (as amended).

Any person who commits any unauthorised act in relation to
this publication may be liable to criminal
prosecution and civil claims for damage.

A CIP catalogue record for this title is
available from the British Library.

ISBN: 978-1-80074-648-0

This is a work of fiction.
Names, characters, places and incidents originate from the writer's
imagination. Any resemblance to actual persons, living or dead, is
purely coincidental.

First Published in 2023

Olympia Publishers
Tallis House
2 Tallis Street
London
EC4Y 0AB

Printed in Great Britain

Dedication

I dedicate my book to my children and my four beautiful granddaughters.

Acknowledgements

I would like to thank my ex-wife, Sue Roberts, for the help she gave to me in writing this book and the proofreading she did for me before submitting it.

EPISODE ONE
The Opening Hole

"Fore" is the shout that I hear as I take off and fly high towards a crowd of spectators, who are eagerly waiting for my arrival.

My name is Li'l Kev. I live my life as a golf ball. I'm very popular and like to be everyone's friend. I love to look very smart and try to do my best to please any Master that wants me to help them.

My Master for the next few days is a six foot, suntanned, athletic kind of guy. He's a cool looking dude who really wants to be everyone's friend but, unlike me, he doesn't know how to. He has an assistant called a Bagman who accompanies him during the next few days. Bagman is an elderly looking man whose Master days are well and truly behind him. He carries the bag of clubs for Master and also offers experience about the upcoming golf courses that may be played. Bagman has a slightly hunched back appearance that reminds me of an old farmer who has carried that one bag of potatoes too many. He will be by my Master's side during the tournament.

So, as I continue my flight, I open my eyes and I know that I'm not going in the right direction. I'm actually gliding over trees instead of the nice landing strip which I'm used to. As I begin to descend, I notice that the spectators start to cover their heads with anything they can get hold of. Some are holding their hands over their heads. I hold my breath as the ground is fast approaching me. I brace myself and pray for a soft landing. I hit the ground and to my amazement didn't feel any pain. It was a soft landing in some kind of thick carpet that I now know as grass. I'm barely seen to the naked eye.

"This feels nice and comfy," I say to myself.

My Master who hit me walks up with the Bagman and tries to hunt me down, I try to bury myself deeper into the long grass. As they get closer, I can see Master has a bad look on his face, I know that I'm in big trouble. Master eventually finds me and gives me a dirty look.

After a brief chat with Bagman, Master decides to pull out a shiny looking club from the bag.

As he takes a couple of practice swings I think to myself, "This is going to hurt!"

Then without warning, Master settles down and it all goes very quiet. I brace myself. Master swings the club. Whoosh! Out I go, flying through the air like the space shuttle taking off. This time I'm heading towards another carpet looking patch of grass. It looks very smooth to me and again I prepare myself for a nice landing.

Thud!

I hit the ground and do a couple of bounces. All of a sudden, I begin to spin backwards just like the Dambusters' bouncing bomb! This makes me feel really dizzy. I slow down, trying to clear my head and came to a standstill.

After stopping, I open my eyes and see what appears to be a hole in the ground. It's the size of a small flowerpot that's been embedded below the surface. If that was my carpet with a hole in it, I'd want it replaced with a new one. Anyhow, someone must have spotted it because somebody had planted a long white pole that's got a flag attached to it!

My Master reaches the carpet area and checks out how near I am to the sunken flowerpot. He picks me up and replaces me with a silver coin. He then throws me to the Bagman who catches me and, get this, without my permission he gives me a good old fashioned scrub down all over with a rough looking towel.

"What's that all about," I think to myself.

Master studies the smooth carpet area and the Bagman returns me back to him. Master places me back down where the silver coin was. He then takes a few steps away from me and I find myself on my own for a few moments. I'm feeling a little uncertain. I cast my eyes around the carpet, there's a hushed crowd of people all staring at me. Master approaches with an awkward looking club called a putter.

"That doesn't look too menacing to me," I think. Master crouches down, then stands tall. I can feel the tension as he offers the putter behind me. It feels like an executioner is waiting to cut my head off! Such drama! Suddenly, he gently swings the putter. I feel relieved as it's a painless contact as I'm on the move towards the sunken pot.

I'm on course and about to drop into it when I say to myself, "Stuff this, I'm not going down there, no way!" I put my brakes on and managed to stop in time. "Phew, that was a close one!"

Before I have a chance to congratulate myself, Master paces up and taps me in the hole anyway. Thank goodness it's only a short fall and that I didn't get hurt. My Master then somehow gets his fingers into the hole and fishes me out. He gives me such a filthy stare then tosses me to the Bagman.

"Don't blame me," I think, "It's not my fault. You're the one that hit me, I didn't want to go down that hole in the first place."

After that, the Bagman yet again gives me another wipe down all over. I now feel as clean as a whistle.

My Master marches angrily on to the next tee box. I like it at this tee box as there is always a nice crowd of spectators gathering around this place. It reminds me of a meeting point for a coffee morning or an auction, it has a friendly feel about it.

On arriving at the tee box, my Master finds me a nice little stool to sit on. I have to make sure I keep my balance as I sit here, otherwise a light gust of wind could blow me off it. But today I feel nice and comfortable and bizarrely relaxed. I even have time to have a good look around at the view. Whilst looking, I notice that there's a sign that says 'Par 5' on it followed by another sign that says '612 yards'.

"That's a long way to fly," I thought.

Master is still feeling angry as he pulls out the biggest, baddest club from out of the bag. It's a real monster! He takes a few steps back away from me and performs a huge swing of the club.

Whoosh. I could feel the venom in that. He does two more swings, both in anger. I can almost feel the power.

Surely he's not going to hit me with that!

Master moves towards me, I start trembling with fear as I wait on my stool for certain impact. I close my eyes. If I had any teeth they would be rattling like mad right now. Then without warning came a loud crack followed by a bang. I've exploded into the air faster than a bullet from a gun. I'm flying as high as a kite and travelling so fast that I can't even open my eyes to see where I'm going. It feels like I'm flying at high speed. Man, what a rush.

After what seems like an age, I experience a falling down feeling. But it's OK, I'm heading towards open land. I can't quite see my landing spot, but I'm fine, dropping downwards faster and faster with incredible speed.

I begin to tense myself and hold my breath at the same time. I'm waiting for a firm impact. Then, suddenly, I hear a splash!

"This feels weird."

I was expecting to experience a few bumps and bounces but I now have a soaking wet feeling. After gathering my senses, I can't believe what my Master had done. He has only hit me into the water. I thought I was already clean enough from when the Bagman gave me a good clean. Why did he need to hit me into the water like that? I'll go straight to the bottom and he knows very well that I can't swim!

After I've been fished out of the water, Master and Bagman decide where I should best be placed on the finer ground. This is where I meet a new friend. His name is Tufty, he is what you call a divot. Tufty is bigger than me, he has a green, hairy fur coat and a brown belly. His size and coat prevent him from flying too high. But he always lands quickly and I say to him how lucky he is. Tufty has many friends on the golf course and I hope to meet some of them in the near future.

So, between Master and Bagman, they are deciding what the next plan of action is to what to do with me. They finally decide to use a long thin looking club that has a knife shaped appearance at one end. This is intended to throw me really high into the air, sending me over what looks like a small, sandy beach and hopefully finishing with a nice soft landing on the smooth carpet area.

"I'm really looking forward to this. I'll be able to keep my eyes open and cannot wait to get a good view of the beach," I think to myself.

My Master strikes. Up I go. But this time my new friend Tufty is going with me. "This is great fun," I say. But, as quickly as Tufty is airborne, he is on his way down and I'm left flying solo again.

As soon as Tufty lands, Master picks him up and places him back to where he took off from. Then, for some reason, my Master decides to tread on his head to make sure that he stays put.

"That's not very nice," I think. Anyway, as I wave farewell to Tufty, I soon begin to descend and eventually land into the smooth carpet area. I actually come to an emergency stop!

"Wow, I never knew that I had so much talent in me. Happy days." I was well chuffed with myself.

I managed to stop very close to the flowerpot hole,

so all my Master needs to do is fetch out his putter and tap me into the hole, which was then followed by a round of applause from the viewing crowd.

This is how things are going to be for the next few days. There will be trials and tribulations, the highs and the lows. To which all will be told at a later date, so for now, we'll fast forward to the last.

EPISODE TWO
The Last Hole

After seventy-one times of being hit off the tee box, I understand that this will be the last time I have to endure the pain. I only know this because I overheard the Bagman tell my Master.

So as I wait patiently perched upon my stool I think to myself, "This is going to be the final time I will be sitting on this stool in this position."

My Master approaches me in a much calmer mood. I find this a little disturbing as I've been used to him being all fired up, angry and business like. He has only one practice swing then strikes me with one of his shiny clubs. This feels strange as I'm normally used to being belted with power and a lot of force.

This time though, I actually enjoy the experience of a much gentler contact. As I take off and glide through the warm air, I find I can open up my eyes and enjoy the views. I even notice the tops of the trees, the watery lakes, the sandy beaches and even the spectators' heads. Sadly, that joy doesn't last too long. Whilst descending towards the ground it looks like I'm going to have a much calmer landing.

The landing is nice and soft, on a spongy piece of lush green carpet. I also have the pleasure of a lovely little roll in the direction of the smoother carpet area. As I slow down and eventually came to a standstill, I hear a ripple of applause from a few spectators standing close by. After stopping, Master and Bagman quickly walk towards me. They both seem very pleased with each other. They even have a smile on their faces and break into gentle laughter. They even got a much bigger round of applause than me!

When they arrive to where I have stopped, they have yet another conversation. I'd seen this many times over the past few days. Goodness knows what they talk about, it beats me! Anyhow, they eventually decide what the best course of action is to take and its great news for me. I'm not going to be hit hard with a big monster club. Instead, I'm just going to have a softer contact that's more like a mild tap on the head.

On this occasion, my Master takes a few more practice swings than normal. He's being more cautious than usual. He steadies himself down and swings the club. I don't feel much contact but I instantly fly high into the air. At this point, I'm delighted to say that I'm accompanied by my new friend. It's Tufty, that patched up piece of green carpet. But, as before and no matter how hard he tries he can never fly and stay in the air as long as me.

This time I don't quite make it to the smooth carpet area. I land just short of it. Luckily, due to my fitness levels and good looks, I put in a final sprint and make it to the smooth zone. As I focused on putting in all that effort to make it there, I forgot to put my brakes on and kept rolling fast towards the flowerpot hole. I'm almost about to fall into it. There's only one thing to do and that's to close my eyes and hope to miss it.

After stopping, I opened my eyes fearing the worse.

"Phew! Result!" I don't know how, but I managed to swerve it just in time, but I'm only a couple of inches away from falling in. To my amazement, I receive a big cheer from all the spectators that surround the carpet.

"Wow! Is that all for me?" I think.

As I'm taking in all the applause, behind me, there is an even bigger cheer and applause. I wonder who that would be for? Well, all that cheering was for my Master. How come he got a bigger cheer than me? I was the one who made the extra effort to get onto the smooth carpet not him. He was miles away.

Anyway, Master and the Bagman continue to take in all of the applause as they step foot onto the carpet area for apparently, the last time. After a mini discussion, they decide to let another Master and Bagman go to play out their match first. Believe it or not, even they get a bigger ovation than I did!

As the applause dies down, the sunlight begins to fade and the shadows seem longer. I notice that the flowerpot hole looks bigger, but I don't know why! My Master steps forward and comes towards me. At that moment, everything goes eerily quiet. Master takes up his position behind me. Everyone in the crowd looks tense, waiting in anticipation for the final climax to take place.

Master then takes a gentle swing with his putter and nudges me into the sunken hole. Plop! Down I go again. That will add up to seventy-two times in a row that I've been in a hole like that.

What follows is a massive roar from all the

spectators. They are clapping and cheering making all sorts of noise. Master throws his cap high into the air and embraces his Bagman.

The crowd are still clapping and cheering, but what about me? I'm still sitting in the hole. I too want to join in the celebrations. Eventually, Master rescues me from the pot hole so now I'm ready to celebrate. But, unknowingly to me, there will be a sting in the tale.

My Master passes me to the Bagman, he wipes me all over with the rough towel again then gives me back to Master. At this point I'm feeling good about myself, but to my surprise and dismay, nothing could prepare me for what happened next.

My Master from somewhere, pulls out a felt tip pen and to my horror, draws on what I can only describe as some sort of graffiti on my head! That's not the end of it, he then decides to toss me into the cheering crowd! I can't believe he did this.

I've spent four long days of being beaten and hit hard seventy-two times from a tee box, seventy-two times been put down a pot hole. I've been in thick grass, buried up to my neck in sand and thrown into bushes and have even been plunged into the water! And this is the thanks I get. Scribbled on my head and thrown away like a used and unwanted toy.

As the celebrations continue, I get caught by a wannabe Master. He told me that I will be saved and put in a special cabinet that's made of glass in his home.

It looks like a sad ending for me as I'll never get to fly again or join in any future celebrations and maybe, not even seen in a children's book. I'll just have to spend the rest of my days being in a display cabinet. But on the upside though, I'll never get hit again, or will I?

So, why don't you come and join me and Tufty for more episodes and adventures on the golf course, we'll have some new friends for you to meet and have fun with!

EPISODE THREE
Meet The Gang!

Now, as promised at the end of the first story, allow me to introduce to you the new friends that me and Tufty have met on the golf course.

Just like most friends that people have, some are good, some are bad, some are loyal and some are sad.

I would imagine that, after I've introduced them to you, there's a possibility that you could find a certain resemblance with your own friends or someone that you may know.

So without further ado, it gives me great pleasure to introduce to you someone who is very special. Her name is Li'l Lizzy.

THE PINK BALL
Li'l Lizzy

Sweet Li'l Lizzy. That is what I call her. When she was born she was bright pink and sparkling, the prettiest ball you could ever wish to see. I like to take care of her and watch over her because she doesn't always have that much good fortune that goes her way. But, as time goes on, her luck is to eventually change for the better.

Li'l Lizzy is someone who tries so hard to do well,

but things never seem to go her way. She always has many different things that she tries her hand at. But as always, she never ever gives up trying at anything.

Then, one day, something happened that would change her life for the better. So watch out for her story. It may just remind you of someone.

THE GOLD BALL
Li'l Daz

Li'l Daz is what you may describe as the golden one. The golden ball. He is made of a material that is called metallic and his golden appearance dazzles everyone.

He doesn't care about any Master that uses him because he knows that he will land perfectly every time. He can bounce off any tree, hit any rock or stone, and it's also been known that he has even skipped over water! (I'm not sure if I believe that one.)

So really, it doesn't matter if he is flying off course or on course, the end result is the same, a perfect landing every time.

The word on the street says that he's even been seen sitting in a sand bunker sunbathing with his shades on! How golden is that! I bet you may have a friend like that!

THE YELLOW BALL
Li'l Timmy

Li'l Timmy, or Timid Timmy as I know him. Li'l Timmy lives a life that is full of fear and worry. He is so frightened of most things, he is quite a scaredy cat. Even if situations haven't even happened yet, he's just scared.

He didn't like the thought of being hit into places such as the long grass or amongst the trees, or any water hazards or sand bunkers. even amongst the spectators. He's definitely afraid of being putted into the flowerpot hole. He says he doesn't like being in the dark! Timmy always thinks that bad things will happen to him and that everything will go wrong for him. He fears that the worst is going to happen every time he's on the golf course. We all worry about Timid Timmy. I wonder if you have a friend like that.

THE RED BALL
Li'l Theo

Li'l Theo is an angry red ball. He's always angry. He was probably born angry. He rants and raves about everything and anything. Nothing seems to make Theo happy. He likes nothing better than to upset everybody and even that still makes him angry.

There's never a smile on his face. If you see him he will always have a grimace on his face and is always spitting venom wherever he goes. He doesn't like anyone that tries to help him and always wonders why nobody wants to be friendly with him.

Eventually, he will find out for himself that being so angry and aggressive will actually not get him anywhere. He will find that nobody wants to be friends with him.

I'm hoping that one day, something will happen to Li'l Theo that will make him change from an angry red ball into a different, mellow one. Fingers crossed for Theo!

THE NO 1 DRIVER
Muggsy

Muggsy is the biggest and baddest club in the golf bag. Nobody messes with Muggsy. He is like the number one doorman of a nightclub. He is the hit you first and ask questions later kind of person.

Everyone freezes when Muggsy comes out of the golf bag. He demands total respect, otherwise there will be consequences to pay. Word of warning, don't mess with Muggsy.

THE PUTTER
Lionel

Lionel usually comes out to play when putting us balls into the flowerpot hole. He never hits any of us hard and he doesn't get angry. He's just not big enough for that, unlike that Muggsy.

Everyone likes to be Lionel's friend because he never wants to hurt us in any way. He is our gentle friend, so I can't understand why any Master wants to throw him around when things don't go as planned.

Lionel doesn't have a single bad bone in him. He has a slightly feminine side to him which makes him look harmless in appearance. He is always well presented and in immaculate condition. It's always nice to have a good friend like Lionel.

THE BUNKER
Sandpit Pete

Last but not least, we have Sandpit Pete. Pete lives in a pile of sand in a crater just in front of the thirteenth hole. He likes to play a game of catch. He sets up his trap and when the moment comes, he springs out of the sand, tries to catch you then buries you deep in the sand. As Masters try to find you, Sandpit Pete acts all innocent and pretends he's not seen anything. Pete thinks it's all very funny; he does laugh a lot to himself. He just has a wicked sense of humour and enjoys annoying any Master who treats us balls badly. We all try to avoid Sandpit Pete because it's not really nice to be buried deep in sand for his entertainment.

So beware of the thirteenth hole! It's always great fun to have a joker in the pack!

EPISODE FOUR
Let's Play Golf

As all good Masters and Bagmen know, it's vitally important to have a good warm up before you start your actual round of golf. Besides doing some stretching exercises to warm up the muscles, you need to hit a few balls around to loosen up so you're ready to play.

So today we will be on a practice ground or, as most people know it, a driving range. Then, after a while on the practice ground, the Masters along with their Bagmen, spend a short time on the specially adapted putting green or, as I call it, the smooth carpet area.

The difference between a normal carpet area on the golf course and the one attached to the practice ground is that there are more flowerpot holes for the Masters to perfect their putting. It's also confusing for us balls because there will be so many of us on the carpet at one time!

Today, a couple of Masters along with their Bagmen have shown up at the practice ground. With the stretching all done, the next thing to do is to decide in a moment when they select their so called practice balls. Some of these balls, in fact, are my friends. This is where I normally get a chance to see and hang out with them.

As I'm pure white in appearance, I'm usually saved

for the actual round of golf. But I just like to hang around the practice area to have a chance to catch up with them. In fact, this is exactly how I met most of my friends in the first place. It's always nice to see them there. We always like a good reunion.

You don't normally see different coloured golf balls on the course, as it's usually the pure white ones like me. But occasionally, due to certain weather conditions, one or two of my friends may be used. Also preparing for a warm up is Muggsy The Driver, and Lionel The Putter. Muggsy looks quite menacing as he flexes his muscles, while Lionel is still taking it easy. He's sitting in the bag. He will be the last one out to do his warm up.

Today, my normal Master for this latest competition decides to select Timmy, The Yellow ball, for his first initial practice strike.

Timmy, as normal, says "I knew he would pick me first!" As always fearing the worse he adds, "I bet he gets Muggsy out of the bag to give me a good old thump!"

Well, Muggsy must have overheard Timmy, because he leaps out of the bag and jumps straight into my Master's hands and he is instantly ready for some action.

As Timmy is nervously waiting, he is perched upon his little stool. You can tell that he is full of fear and worry. But to my amazement and Timmy's, my Master changes his mind and puts Muggsy back into the bag and instead, he asks his Bagman to pass him a much less aggressive club. Muggsy is back in the bag and he is steaming and fuming with anger. He was dying to throw his weight around. For now, Timmy is let off the hook.

It's typical of him. He has all that fear and worry for

nothing. I really hope he stops feeling like that. His life will be much more pleasant if he has a better positive mind set. I cannot help but worry about Li'l Timmy. He's such a good friend and you will find out why later on.

Not far from the practice area lays a patch of ground that looks like a smooth green carpet. It has a few more flowerpot holes than the ones that are on the golf course. This is where I can usually find my good friend Lionel, The Putter, having a warm up. Lionel loves it here; it's all nice and relaxed with no pressure involved.

On the carpet today is Li'l Lizzy, The Pink Ball. She is joined by Li'l Daz, The Gold Ball. But! Wait for it! There is also Li'l Theo, The Red Ball.

Today's Master is not my usual one. My usual one is still on the main practice area. I thought I'd pop over to the smooth carpet area to see my other friends. This Master is nothing special – he is just a mediocre player – but he's always there amongst the other mediocre players. In fact he happens to be my Master's good friend and today he asked my Master if he could borrow Lionel, The Putter, for a few minutes practice.

Straight away, this angers Li'l Theo!

"No surprise there!" I say to myself.

Lionel's first task is to give Li'l Lizzy a nice gentle tap towards the first flowerpot hole. She's about twelve feet away.

"Don't worry," says Lionel. "I won't hurt you."

So tap! Contact is made. Li'l Lizzy is on her way, strolling along in her bright pink outfit.

Unfortunately, she doesn't quite make it to the flowerpot hole. It's no matter how hard she tries, she can never make it to the flowerpot hole in one attempt. The story of her life you might say! But, she never gives up trying! Even when she doesn't want to try anymore, she will still try. Time after time I've seen her fail, but, I can't wait for the day when her luck will eventually change for the better.

The next ball Lionel will tap is going to be Li'l Daz The Gold Ball. He too is around twelve feet away from the same flowerpot hole as Li'l Lizzy. So as Lionel approaches him, the sun decides to pop out and shines straight on Li'l Daz, making his golden coat glisten brighter than ever! Lionel then gives him a little tap. "Damn it", says Lionel "I don't think I've tapped him hard enough. This Master won't be happy with me!"

"Have no fear" says Li'l Daz. "Watch me go, Lionel". And with that, Li'l Daz puts in a big sprint and rushes towards the flowerpot hole. As if by magic, he gleefully plops down the hole and shouts, "Touchdown!" That is then followed up by a celebratory dance.

Poor Li'l Lizzy. She would love to be like Li'l Daz. She sighs as she carries on watching his celebration dance.

Next up it's Li'l Theo, The Red Ball. Lionel is definitely not looking forward to this. The Master decides to place Li'l Theo at least a good thirty feet away from the same flowerpot hole. That means poor Lionel has to give Li'l Theo a much firmer tap than the others.

This angers Li'l Theo, as you can imagine. It frightens him a little bit.

"Don't you dare even think about hitting me hard," barks Li'l Theo. "Why don't you go back into your bag and leave me alone? I don't want to play with you today, so go away!"

This clearly upsets Lionel but, unfortunately, the Master forces him to tap Li'l Theo towards the flowerpot hole. Lionel closes his eyes and firmly pushes Li'l Theo towards the hole.

"Get out of my way!" Li'l Theo screams as he races away.

He is just about to fall into the flowerpot hole when he does a massive swerve and rolls away to the left of it.

"That's good enough for me," says Li'l Theo. "I hope they leave me alone now. Who wants to be friends with them anyway? Not me!"

He is still seething and muttering in his own way as he storms off. What an angry red ball he is!

EPISODE FIVE
The Thirteenth Hole

The thirteenth hole is a very special place to be. It's home to someone called Sandpit Pete. Pete lives in the bunker that's just in front of the smooth carpet area.

This is where Pete likes to play tricks and hides any golf ball who threatens his special space. He loves to do it for his own entertainment and fun.

The thirteenth hole is a long par five and many a Master is very nervous about playing on the thirteenth. It's normally around six hundred and twelve yards from start to finish.

I'm out with my usual Master and Bagman today and I know what's about to come my way. As it's the longest journey I have to take, I know I'll have to come face to face with, yes, well, you have guessed it, it's Muggsy the driver.

This is the moment that Muggsy thrives on. He won't care how hard he hits you or where you're going to land, he just wants to unleash his raw power.

So, as my Master and Bagman approach the tee box at the start of the thirteenth hole, I start to feel a little bit uneasy. Muggsy is getting all pumped up and ready to rumble. Even the Bagman is feeling nervous about what Muggsy is about to do!

Muggsy doesn't ask any questions, he lets other people do that. This brute of a golf club can, and will, deliver a devastating blow that any ball will do well to survive. So, with all that in mind, I calmly await my fate whilst I sit down on my made-to-measure stool.

I decide to put my game face on and summon up some courage to brace myself for what's about to come my way. Try and look at it this way, it's a David and Goliath situation. I have faced it many, many times before. I'm ready now for the challenge. Wishful thinking, springs to mind!

As Muggsy is finally selected out of the bag, he fully knows that he has a job to do. My master feels the power in his hands as he does a couple of practice swings.

Muggsy is now chomping at the bit and is ready for action. He is ready and so am I. I can hear let's get ready to rumble in my head. My Master does a huge swing. There's an explosion of power and, weirdly, I don't feel anything.

Muggsy must hit me in the right spot. It's like a boxer being delivered a knockout blow; you can't feel it, but it puts you down on the canvas or in my case, the fairway.

I had no idea about the flight, but I wake up on the soft grass. The first person I see when I open up my eyes is my good friend Tufty. He asks me if I'm OK.

I'm so happy to see a friendly face. While I am waiting for my Master and Bagman to arrive, I have a great chance to catch up and touch base with my old mate Tufty.

As you know, Tufty has a simple life. I know that he can't fly very well, but he does live in the best place on the golf course. I just wish all those Master's would stop putting their feet on him and flattening him into the ground.

As my Master catches up with me, I get ready to part ways with Tufty. I still have a long flight to go to get onto the smooth carpet area. It will take another hefty blow from my Master. But that's not my main worry. My real concern is getting past Sandpit Pete.

As my Master walks up to me, he steps on poor Tufty quite heavily. Most Masters do this just to make sure that he stays in place. My Master and Bagman assess the situation to decide the appropriate action so that I get onto the smooth carpet area. Do they take a chance and go for it in one hit, or do they try and place me nearby to avoid any trouble? Remember, there's always a risk when a brave attempt is tried. Make a note of that, reader!

As I'm sitting in what appears to be in a good location, for my money, my choice would be to play it safe and avoid any danger. Unfortunately for me, the law of extremes has come into play. My Master is going for it. The gamble is on. It's in the lap of the gods for me right now.

Now, this is the situation. I have nearly two hundred and fifty yards flight time to go. Master and Bagman think it's worth a gamble to land me on the smooth carpet area with one good clean strike. The only danger to worry about is negotiating getting past Sandpit Pete.

Bagman picks a mid-range unnamed club from the bag.

I'm thinking, "Thank goodness it's not Muggsy." I've already survived that experience!

My Master settles down. He does a super fast swing and off I go. It was that fast, I didn't even have enough time to say farewell to Tufty.

Now I'm flying high and I'm bang in line to land on the smooth carpet area. As I start my descent, I can clearly see my landing spot and the faster I'm descending, it seems like everything is going to plan.

I'm preparing for a nice smooth landing, when all of a sudden and right out of the blue, a giant hand made of sand reaches out of the sandpit and plucks me right out of the air. May I also add, it was done in one swift swoop and in a split second.

I'm now instantly buried deep into the sand, followed by someone saying, "Got you," ringing in my ears. It is Sandpit Pete.

Sandpit Pete has struck again and it's me this time. I can hear giggling and laughter. It's like being the victim of the Joker out of the Batman films. Sandpit Pete has been fed and is well happy with himself while I'm feeling sad in the sand.

As my Master and Bagman show up at the scene, they both ask Sandpit Pete for my whereabouts.

"I've seen no sign of him," Pete says. "Why don't you take a look in that long grass over there?"

Master and Bagman follow Pete's advice and take a good look around with no luck in finding me. They are just about to give up and concede that I'm a lost ball and prepare to play another one, when all of a sudden, Pete decides to spit me out and I'm into play again.

He shouts out laughingly, "Fooled you all!"

Master and Bagman look bemused. I'm relieved. The crowd are in fits of laughter. Another one at the mercy of Pete's comedy. That's Sandpit Pete for you!

EPISODE SIX
A Time For A Change

Well, reader, I hope that you've all kept up with the pace so far. Now I need to tell you about the time that some of my friends have, let's just say, changed their ways.

So firstly, I'd like to tell you about the day Li'l Lizzy's fortunes changed for the better. As you know, Li'l Lizzy is one of nature's best little triers. She always gives it one hundred per cent effort. But, often she still fails to find success. Then, one day when she was least expecting it, something happened to change her life for the better.

This was in a time when several Masters were about to go out to get some practice on the putting green, or as I know it, the smooth carpet area with extra flowerpot holes. It was an overcast day and most of the Masters with their Bagmen had their wet weather clothes on. My Master and his usual Bagman also had their waterproofs on as the weather forecast was really a mixture of sunshine and occasional showers.

After a quick chat amongst each other, it was time to select their practice balls. As there was a little bit of a chill in the air, most of the practice balls were all huddled together to keep warm. My friends were also in that bunch. There was Li'l Timmy, Li'l Daz, Lil Lizzy and a certain ball that was kicking up a fuss, Li'l Theo.

Li'l Theo was being his normal self, pushing and shoving the other balls out of the way, also cursing at everyone at the same time. It is hard for me to watch the behaviour of Li'l Theo, as he mostly acts like a hard boiled sweet, but I'd like to think that he does have a soft centre inside. Hopefully, I'll see that one day.

Anyhow, let's get back to Li'l Lizzy. A strange moment happened and I was lucky enough to see it. As you know at this point, I'm normally saved for the main event due to my immaculate white suit, so that's why I have time on my hands to catch up with my friends.

As the other Masters chose their practice balls, it was now time for my Master to select his. As he was about to make his choice, the sun burst out a ray of sunlight which shined straight onto Li'l Lizzy. Her coat became the brightest pink colour that you could ever see. She stood out from all the other balls like the brightest star in the sky. Shining bright, like a diamond.

My Master says to his Bagman, "I'm having this ball today." He then added, "This beautiful little pink ball is the prettiest one in the bunch, let's see if it gives me any luck."

I was so pleased as I looked on, that my Master has chosen Li'l Lizzy for his practice ball. I just hoped and prayed that this would work out for her. This also meant that my Master would have me for the main event and Li'l Lizzy for practice on the smooth carpet area. How cool is that!

The only thing left for us to do was to perform to the best of our ability.

So, it was time for Li'l Lizzy to face her biggest test,

not only for my Master, but for herself. The last thing that she wanted to do was to let my Master down. He is probably the best Master out of all the others. She certainly did not want to let herself down either.

Now was the moment for Li'l Lizzy to show what she can do. My Master placed her around ten feet away from the first flowerpot hole. He decided what to use. He then pulled out a friendly face from out of his bag. It was only Lionel, The Putter, and he's our good friend. He would do his utmost best to help out Li'l Lizzy.

My Master got ready with Lionel and approached Li'l Lizzy. I'm watching on nervously. I could feel a knot in my tummy. My Master slowly swung Lionel and tapped Li'l Lizzy towards the first flowerpot hole. Away she went. Her speed looked too slow and she was drifting off-line. Oh no! I couldn't look. I had to close my eyes. All of a sudden, I heard 'plop'. I took a look.

"YES" I cried out. "Yes!" She had made it at the first try. I was happy for her.

My Master walked over and picked her out of the flowerpot hole. He was so pleased and Li'l Lizzy had the biggest smile you have ever seen.

But things didn't stop there. Hole after hole, she made all of them in one go. And no matter what the distance was, five, ten, twenty and even thirty feet away, she made all of those distances.

My Master was so over the moon with her, he was elated. He told his Bagman that he wanted to use Li'l Lizzy all the time for his practice warm ups. Li'l Lizzy will now be looked after by the best Master, and on the best smooth carpet area from now on.

Li'l Lizzy had finally got the success that she had been trying so hard for. And now, she will be living the life that she deserves to live, with the Master.

So, reader, that could be a little lesson for all of us to go by, never give up, because you can get what you're looking for in the end! (With a bit of help from Lionel of course!)

I'll never forget about the time that Li'l Theo, changed for the better. That too was a strange occasion. It was when all of us golf balls were on the practice, smooth carpet area with all those extra flowerpot holes.

There was Li'l Lizzy, fresh from her last visit, and looking the happiest that I've ever seen her. There was also Li'l Timmy, Li'l Daz and Li'l Theo. Even I was given a chance to join them and have a little get together with Lionel.

It was a nice sunny day which made all of our suits look lovely, bright and clean. On this occasion, we all had a different Master. Everything seemed to be going really well. We were all having fun together. We were all being tapped around the practice, area where some of us were being putted into the flowerpot hole in one attempt, especially Li'l Daz, and now so does Li'l Lizzy, with her new found good fortune.

Me, along with Li'l Timmy and Li'l Theo, were having some near misses trying to get down the flowerpot holes, so, it was really great to be on the smooth carpet area at the same time.

Li'l Theo was waiting to be picked up by his Master. He had just missed being putted in the chosen flowerpot hole, when Lionel accidentally tapped Li'l Timmy towards the same hole.

Before Li'l Theo could be picked up, there was a smack. Li'l Timmy just collided straight into him, sending Li'l Theo spinning and rolling away.

"You stupid idiot," screamed Li'l Theo as he came to a standstill. "What did you do that for you useless yellow ball."

This really upset Li'l Timmy He's not used to being shouted at like that.

Me, Li'l Daz, and even Li'l Lizzy, all shouted.

"Steady on Theo!" I said to him. "Timmy couldn't help it, he didn't bump into you on purpose."

But that didn't cut any ice with Li'l Theo. He went into a right meltdown, cursing not just at Li'l Timmy, but also at the rest of us, including poor Lionel. You could see steam coming out of Li'l Theo, and this little red ball was getting more and more angry than ever before.

The final straw came when Li'l Theo, at the peak of losing his temper, screamed at all of us at the top of his voice, "GET LOST, THE LOT OF YOU. That includes you, Lionel!"

Poor Lionel was aghast.

Just as Li'l Theo started to storm off, and before he got too far, an unexpected voice sounded out towards Li'l Theo's direction. It simply said, "That's enough!"

Li'l Theo spun around. That voice came from Li'l Timmy! None of us expected that. We were all shocked, and Li'l Theo was stunned.

This was so out of character for Li'l Timmy. He has always been quiet, shy and not the type to have an outburst or upset anyone. Something must have hit a raw nerve, and that something was an angry red ball that goes by the name of Li'l Theo.

As Li'l Theo stood and glared at Li'l Timmy, Li'l Timmy retaliated. "I've had enough of you Theo! Me and all the others have all tried to be nice to you, and all you do in return is to be horrible and nasty to all of us and that now includes poor Lionel."

He added, "Theo, I'm done with putting up with all of your tantrums and anger, so from now on, I don't want to be your friend anymore!"

This outburst totally stunned Li'l Theo. He has never known Li'l Timmy to be like that. Li'l Theo has always had a soft spot for Li'l Timmy. Without showing it, Li'l Theo would watch over and protect him like a good friend would do. Now he was in danger of losing the only friend that he really cared about.

Still stunned by what Li'l Timmy said, Li'l Theo just stood there in silence. For once he didn't know what to do. But, he did do the only thing that he could do, and that was to stand still and burst into tears. None of us have ever seen Li'l Theo cry like that. None of us have ever seen Li'l Timmy stand up for himself like that either.

We can all learn that being angry all of the time doesn't really get you anywhere, because you may lose the people that care about you the most. Just ask Li'l Theo.

After that scene was over, that became the signal for things to change. Li'l Lizzy's fortune finally got better. Li'l Timmy discovered that he had a voice and had the confidence to stand up for himself, as well as letting go of all his fears and worries. Li'l Theo realised that being angry all of the time will only make him be alone and have no friends. And as for me, with taking all this in, there was only one thing to do and that is, LET'S ALL HAVE A HOLIDAY!

EPISODE SEVEN
Let's Have A Holiday

Well, after all that had happened in the last episode, I decided that we could all do with a nice break. So, where would you say a group of all different coloured golf balls would go out for a holiday?

To my mind, there's only one place to go to have a fun time and let off some steam. So, let's all go to the seaside and go crazy. Yes, let's all go crazy golf! I know it's not everyone's cup of tea, but, for us different coloured golf balls, it's the perfect choice.

Unfortunately, some of the gang can't come with us on this trip as it's for golf balls only. So that will be, Li'l Lizzy, Li'l Daz, Li'l Timmy, the new ex-angry ball Li'l Theo and of course myself. We will try and see if Lionel will be allowed to join us, but that decision belongs to my Master.

As for Sandpit Pete and Tufty, I'm afraid they will not be able to leave the golf course, which is a shame. We won't tell Muggsy. He knows that big drivers like him are not allowed on a crazy golf course, so he will probably be angry with us when we return.

I know it sounds weird that a set of five golf balls and a putter will be going on holiday to the seaside to play crazy golf but, reader, why don't we all use our imagination and pretend that they can?

Picture those little golf balls, all dressed in Hawaiian shirts of all colours with sunglasses on, and backpacks on their backs. The putter is disguised as an umbrella. How good will that be!

Let's let our imagination come to life, my small gang of friends are going on holiday to the seaside. Think of how much joy that we can bring to people of all ages, young or old. Everybody at some stage has been to the seaside to play crazy golf and had fun and my group of friends are going to make sure that they do.

Me and my friends always like to play crazy golf. For us, it means that we can do whatever we wanted do. We don't have to do as we are told, and we can get up to all kinds of mischief. We can ping around holes made of concrete which makes us go faster, just like in a pinball machine. We can hide in windmills, small houses and even play tricks by deliberately bouncing out of holes.

Everyone loves to play crazy golf. My friends and myself are like the people who play the game; we have as much fun as the people who play with us. They have fun and so do we, it's an amazing feeling to bring happiness and laughter to everyone.

Our first day of crazy golf was brilliant. All of us were picked out to play at the same time. Lionel was also picked, what a great start!

We were picked out by a family of five, three young children and two adults. It was a sunny day, so we all had our sunglasses on. Imagine, how cool we all looked.

The first of us to go was me, of course. I would be showing the rest of the golf balls the route to the hole.

The route on this hole is more like a Grand Prix track. It had snake-like bends, so the idea was to bounce off the bendy walls and head towards the hole.

Lionel was used first and he gently tapped me towards the first bend. I hit the wall and bounced away with incredible speed. So, now I was in a pinball mode. It was fantastic. I was bouncing away with not knowing where I was going next. I must have bounced over the hole at least half a dozen times! Eventually, I came to a stop. I was not too far from the hole. That was one cool ride!

Li'l Lizzy was next to go and Lionel was used again. Li'l Lizzy took the same route as me. She was loving it, screaming and laughing all the way. She was just passing me, and as she did, she clipped into me sending me spinning away and deflected herself straight into the hole.

"Yes!" said Lionel. Everyone else cheered too. She was down in one. I told you her luck had changed! Maybe I should start calling her Lucky Liz.

Next to go was Li'l Daz. Again, Lionel was used and again, the same route was chosen. Li'l Daz, golden as ever, really picked up his speed. He was heading straight for the hole. But, for some odd reason, a gust of wind picked up and blew me towards the hole. I collided into Li'l Daz, causing him to completely miss the hole!

"Oops! Sorry, I didn't mean for that to happen."

Li'l Daz was fine about it. He didn't care, because he was on holiday, and he still thinks he is the golden one, even if he had just missed!

Li'l Timmy and Li'l Theo started off together.

"This could be trouble." I thought. They were hit by

the young children and were both taking different routes towards the hole. They were pinging around, pinball style, narrowly missing each other. I had to close my eyes in case they bumped into each other. I'm still not a hundred per cent certain that Li'l Theo has changed his ways. He still may be an angry red ball.

Well, their journey seemed to go on and on with no sign of slowing down the fast pace. In fact, it was really lucky that neither of them never bumped into me. At their pace, I would have been completely knocked straight out of the track!

As I was still trying my best to keep out of the way, yes, you've guessed it, there was a crash. They both bounced off separate walls and headed straight towards each other. They collided like bumper cars sending them both bouncing and spinning around in different directions.

Me and the others were expecting a big outburst from Li'l Theo. To all our amazement, Li'l Theo just burst into fits of laughter, saying, "Wow, that was great fun."

Then, with Li'l Timmy being a natural worrier and us believing he could be thinking that he had upset or hurt Li'l Theo, stunned us as well, when he also burst out laughing. This was unbelievable. A little while ago, you would have never seen that from those two. It looked like the change had done them both good.

So, that set the tone for the rest of the holiday. We had lots of fun amongst ourselves. So did the people who played with us. And the most important thing to learn about this experience, is that if a small tiny golf ball had the ability to change, then so can people. We don't all need to be angry with everything, or be worried and in fear of things. Not everyone can be golden, but you can be golden if you keep trying and don't give up!

We all have our own dreams to follow, even I do. Mine is simply to enjoy life, even if it is through a golf ball's eyes. You never know, maybe one day, my story will be told or even be made into an animated television series. Maybe me and my friends will be made into cuddly toys.

As I sit in my display cabinet waiting for my dreams to come true, I hope yours come true too. But what do I know, I'm just a golf ball who goes by the name of Li'l Kev.